Love is the Key

MESSAGES OF LOVE AND GUIDANCE CHANNELLED FROM

THE CIRCLE OF THE LIGHT BY KAY MEADE

Kay Meade & Peter Ashley

Copyright © 2012   Kay Meade and Peter Ashley
Earth Message Press
earthmessagepress@clear.net.nz
www.earthmessagepress.com

ISBN   978-0-473-20652-9

Cover illustrations   *Rachel Auton, Lotus Lifestyle, Brisbane*
                         Denise Durkin, Illustration Wish, Wellington
Copy editing and design   *Flying Frog®, Paraparaumu Beach*

This book is dedicated to those countless spiritual beings - guides, helpers and angels, who watch over us and work tirelessly to care for humankind and Mother Earth

Purpose of The Circle of The Light

" The Circle of The Light of The Love Energy has a significant role to play in reconnecting the Love Energy that was seeded on the Earth many years ago."

" We are giving wisdom and nurture. It is our role to give, to teach, to help all on Earth. In our giving we hope and intend to release from the centre of your being the Light that dwells within."

" These messages are full of divine knowledge and wisdom and will harken the awakening of the masses. That is the desired affect that we seek."

— *From The Circle of The Light of The Love Energy*

Foreword

Much to my surprise I started to channel for the first time during a session at a meditation group in 2009. A group energy spoke through me and began to give the most beautiful messages about love and light. I have been channelling this group energy since then. In a later session at home with just Peter and myself they introduced themselves as the Circle of The Light of The Love Energy – the purest energy of all. The story of this introduction is told in our first book of their messages *Earth Messages of the Love Energy*.

Different things move us on our spiritual journey and make us curious to explore. What made me search more was the break-up of my 28-year marriage. However, this story started long before.

When I was a teenager and also as a young adult I experienced a few out-of-body experiences. One such experience took me back to my college and I saw my marked English exam paper with 1st on it. This surprised me. The next day at English the teacher dropped my paper on my desk and as she walked away she said " 64%". I had a sinking feeling that my evening experience was not for real. But then the teacher said in a not so pleased voice, "and that's first". I was pleased, as it confirmed my 'secret' experience.

At times I could see auras around people. This often happened at the most unexpected times.

I questioned why we are here and believed there must be more to this life, that there must be a purpose. In discussing this with friends one night at a restaurant – one of them said I needed to meditate. He took me to the group where he meditated and this was a beginning. Some years later I was taken by another friend to the Spiritualist Church, and eventually joined a development group or 'circle' for a short period of time.

Before my marriage break-up I had been diagnosed with an illness and told that I would need to take prescription medicine for the rest of my life. I took the medicine for a short while but had lots of side effects. This is when I explored natural health, spiritual healing and reiki. Another friend then told me of a meditation group and it was in this group that I started to see, with my third eye, a face appear. For months after that, every time I meditated I saw just a pair of bright wise eyes, then gradually the nose and mouth – it looked like a mask.

The lady running this group then moved to Australia and the group closed. But I continued to meditate. Eventually I saw the whole face complete with wrinkles, hair and beard. Two more faces appeared in later meditation sessions. One was the face of a young woman with a veil over her head, no hair showing. Her picture is on the cover of this book and was drawn by Rachael Auton, a physic artist. The other image presented was a man with the most beautiful compassionate eyes and gentle manner.

This is when I again felt the need to join a development circle at a Spiritualist Church to learn more about the part of me that is spirit. I don't know exactly what I expected to learn, but it wasn't to go into trance and have spirit talk through me! The first time this happened, my whole body felt full of energy and tingled during the entire transmission. My voice and mannerisms changed. I did not remember what was said, but I will always remember the amazing electric feelings.

The others present told me that a wise-sounding being spoke through me in a powerful male voice, and that I was bent over like an old and frail man leaning on a staff. I shook and swayed from side to side. The others in the group were too occupied with trying to catch me if I fell, so not much notice was taken of what I actually said.

As I continued to meditate, I received more messages. They said that they wanted to keep the messages simple and that information would be given in small stages. The messages given invariably finished with "please pass this message on". So with my wonderful supportive partner Peter recording and transcribing the messages, this second book is born.

Both Peter and I are quiet by nature and would prefer to be in the background. So it took some soul searching to produce the first, and now this second book.

The messages are consistent and persistent – a plea for *love* to be on Earth – and this request is presented in many ways. Despite our desire for privacy, both Peter and I feel so moved by these pleas that we feel compelled to pass them on so fellow seekers can share the guidance and messages of love.

When compiling this book we wondered whether to include all the messages, as some could be seen as repetitive. Yet in some way the messages each seem to introduce another facet on how to implement their requests or consider putting them into practice, so all are included.

Our journey has opened up the field of energy healing and teaching to us. We are both Reiki Master Teachers and enjoy channelling this healing energy to others. Peter has recently completed the advanced training for Dolores Cannon's

Quantum Healing Hypnosis Therapy and is using this technique on willing volunteers with good results.

We now run our own weekly meditation group and it is wonderful to feel the energy increase, providing nurture to the part of us that is spirit. This is a world we would never have thought we would be entering just a few years ago.

We would encourage readers to start their own meditation group, or join an existing meditation group. It is a great way to tune into the energy of pure love and to discover more about your spirituality.

Peter has now created a website for the messages I receive. In future, selected messages will be posted to our blog on this website. Please use the 'Follow Blog by Email' facility on www.earthmessagepress.com to subscribe and receive the messages promptly by email.

Read the messages with an open heart and see what resonates for you.

We hope you will find it possible to help Earth and humanity by raising the energy of pure love in your thoughts and actions in life.

Love and Light.

— *Kay Meade*

The symbol

Kay was given this symbol to help her connect to The Circle of The Light of The Love Energy. You too can use it during meditation. Visualise the symbol at your third eye and keep your focus on it to help you with your spirit guide connections.

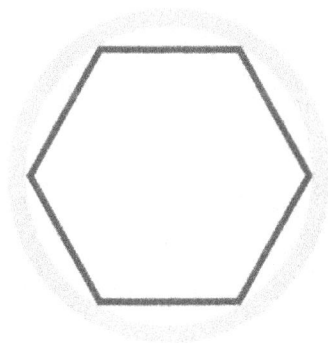

Contents

Introduction

This book continues with the messages of love and guidance first presented in our earlier book *Earth Messages of the Love Energy*. The messages are channelled by Kay Meade, a New Zealand-based trance medium, from a group of beings in the higher spiritual realms who call themselves 'The Circle of The Light of The Love Energy'. They say they wish to spread and increase the energy of love on Earth.

Kay does not remember what she has said during channelling. Her words are recorded electronically and later transcribed. The original emotion is not so apparent when the messages are transcribed, nor is the emphasis on certain words.

Occasionally Kay will feel that she needs to write a message, rather than bringing it through in the trance state.

Most of these messages were received in 2011, and they are presented in approximate chronological order. Each message has been categorised into the chapter it most suits. The three chapters are 'Love and guidance', 'Earth changes and transition' and 'Spiritual poetry'. Because the content of a message is often wide ranging, decisions on classification have sometimes been arbitrary.

English is by no means the first language of the members of The Circle of The Light of The Love Energy, so the grammar is sometimes imperfect and some words are used in an unusual way. To preserve authenticity, there has been minimal editing.

Some of the messages were received at Kay and Peter's

weekly meditation group or 'circle' and need to be read with that in mind.

Kay channels several different spiritual guides who have distinct voices, personalities and mannerisms. They say their help and love will be freely given, if only we would ask.

They see these messages as a catalyst for change, helping the transition to a world based on love.

Feedback from The Circle of The Light

We published the first book of messages early in 2011. In December 2010, when we had a completed draft of the book cover design and wording, Kay channelled the following message from The Circle of The Light of The Love Energy.

We are greatly pleased with the presentation and depiction of the words in the cover of 'our' book.

It is very rewarding for us to see that the task that has been given to you has been taken seriously and is manifesting in this form. Our words can now reach all those who seek. The sincerity of task is seen by all in The Circle of The Light of The Love Energy.

This our gift to all Earth beings will give guidance, allowing all who read this gift such an opportunity of fulfilment. This is the beginning, this is where the expansion begins and then the golden rain will give nourishment and Light. The golden rain will form a network that will connect Earth to heaven. It is like a web, all parts connect.

Kay broke from channelling the message to explain. "I see all the golden filaments going longitudinally and latitudinally around Earth, creating an outer frame that surrounds the Earth. It is away from the Earth, it is sort of like a protective layer, it is set out from the Earth and it goes all around it and that way as well." While talking Kay used hand gestures to illustrate. She then continued channelling.

And that is what is going to happen when all work from the heart base. They are making connection with the

Heavens above and they are forming a shield of love around the Earth. This will be a protective barrier between negative energies and this needs to be in place – this barrier – for the preparation of the time of the Great Magnificence – Earth needs to be at one with the energies of love.

Love and guidance

This section contains messages of guidance for spiritual development and enlightenment.

As mentioned earlier, many of these messages were addressed to our weekly meditation group, or 'circle' and need to be read with that in mind.

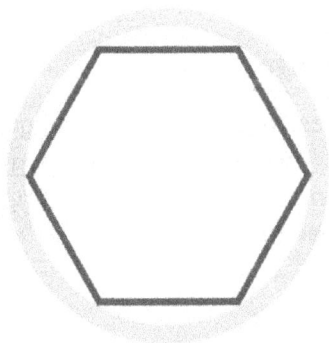

New morning

Feel the calmness of the new morning greet you with much love and hope. Feel the new energy greet your beingness this morning as the awakening of the purpose of the soul is manifested.

Pathway to enlightenment

All steps on the pathway to enlightenment are to be taken knowing that the faith you have will be steadfastly guiding you through.

All happenings in life need to be accepted with love, then all will be resolved with love.

Walking your path

Walking a path outside of the expected may be seen as difficult, but we are with you, and we are helping you, and all the support that you need is with you. Keep walking the path.

Working with spirit

When working with spirit it is not unreasonable to feel amazing, strange, unusual sensations and see and sense and hear things that you haven't before.

Don't feel bewildered, just trust in the divine. Feel and sense the emotion. Ask why you feel this way. Spirit will answer.

Pure energy of love

The pure energy of love will provide the physical being solace, understanding, and harmony that in turn will nourish the spirit, soul, essence within with the knowledge of who they are and why they came to the Earth plane. Awakening the spirit, soul, essence connection to the *source* and activating the love energy on Earth.

Behold the Light

Behold the Light (*Kay was stretching out a cupped hand*). The Light penetrates all life and it is a wonder to behold.

The Light shines even more brightly now and will become even brighter in the coming days.

The thinning of the veil will allow this Light to shine more brightly in all awakened souls on Earth and confirmation of task will be known and acknowledged by many.

The Light is so important at this time. It is the forerunner for the Great Magnificence. A time of great enlightenment is upon the Earth.

The God force

Every time you are with your family or in nature, see and appreciate all there is in that situation. Draw from the situation, so that you build on what you have been learning. See the God force in all of those things because the God force is in everything and needs to be seen to be appreciated.

Appreciate what you have because you have much. You have so much wealth and richness within you to share with those around you in everything you do.

Let your riches pour out to help your family, your friends, your colleagues, your associates. Let it spread. It is so important to let the goodness within you spread around all those and all the things that you touch and do. Do this and you will connect with your guides and the God force within.

Always feel the God force because it is so strong and it needs to be shown to all at this time. Keep it in the forefront in every situation – good, bad – bring the God force forth. The positive will always reign!

Ben Joseph

When BenJoseph (son of Joseph) walked the Earth, times were very dark, no sparks of Light were very apparent.

There were groups set up to be there for his arrival and he walked his path learning and trusting, and this is what is asked of all who walk the Earth.

He had the same frailties, but his faith and his trust were foremost in his life. Each individual who enters Earth's realm needs to find the faith and the trust, just like he did.

The seeds were planted in his time and they still grow in those who are awakened to the Light. Those who are awakened need now to spread out and let their learning and their faith and their trust be ever so foremost in their daily lives.

The continuation of the evolution of the spirit is at a juncture and it is on the rising.

Passing over

The spirit leaves the body before the anguish and the pain that the human imagines about the scene of the passing. I hope that is clear.

The human form is just the coating

The human form is just consequential to the important part within.

The human form is just the coating and does not show the true essence within the body.

Healing the essence

It is not the physical body that needs healing. It is the spirit, soul, the very essence of the humanness, and the physical will then be healed.

Help us by healing the very essence, what is within the humanness that needs our healing to restore health balance to be at one.

Let each discover at their own level

In peace and in love I come. As do all in The Circle of The Light. The energy of love, as you have been told by us before, is the key to all situations on Earth.

The messages have been given and it is with thanks that we see them being circulated. The messages do hold information of value to all. All who read will at least question, even if they don't comprehend initially.

Do not be discouraged, but let those who read open their eyes to possibilities. Without the possibilities there is no hope of discovery.

Let each person discover at their own level. That is all that is asked and the completion of the book (*Earth Messages of the Love Energy*) is the beginning for many.

Love is the key

We come in love to give hope. Love is the key.

All events that take place, take place with a purpose and the purpose is to awaken the soul to the purpose of its being on the Earth.

In the awakening all good will prevail. It will allow all of the love to heal all of the world.

The answer is with each human being. It knows its purpose, but it does so easily get sidetracked.

Encourage all to focus on the purpose. The purpose is what will allow Earth to prevail.

Appreciate opportunities

Oh please appreciate all that you have been given. Feel
and see and know that those opportunities are part of
your path.

Explore the opportunities as they will give you the
satisfaction of discovering and nourishing the spirit, the
soul. Your path will be completed when the full expansion
of the opportunities is taken.

Place no restrictions on yourself

We urge all to place no restrictions or limitations on their journey in life.

Embrace the freedom of the times you live. Allow yourselves to unfold and expand.

Accept that whatever your journey in life presents unto you:

• it is worthwhile

• it is meant to be

• it is what you asked for and agreed to

• it is part of your blueprint

• it is possible to meet anything you see as a challenge.

What is impossible to the mind is possible to the spirit. There are no limitations, so do not allow the mind to limit your experience in life.

Be in the freedom of your time and be the divine being that you are. See everything as being good for you. Find freedom in adversity and you will be truly free.

Actions to be expressed in love

Let the action of your being be an expression of who you are. Let every deed that you undertake be an expression of yourself – the love that you are – and let the action be expressed in love, understanding, harmony with all.

Stand in your Light

Your Light will attract all of the things that you need, but you need to 'Stand in your Light'.

Do not let others interrupt what you want to do and be. In the Light you are open, you are a true expression of yourself and you need to be open to allow what you need to be given.

See the pathway with all its guiding lights and read the symbols so that you can stand in your Light. Your Light will help to bring to you what you are here to do.

Keep following the path. It is lit to show you the way.

What you are meant to have

With every step you take, let your love flow from you to all who you come in contact with. With your hands spread love and with your voice give thanks and love. Let your eyes see in every situation the good there is on your Earth.

When you look at things like that you will be able to see that what has been created for you provides everything you need. When you eliminate from your plane the negativity that is so harmful, you will have what you are meant to have.

Investment in the inner self

Many words of guidance have been given and knowledge of abundance within has been given. It is time to invest in the abundance that is within. It is the only thing that is important.

Everything that you need is within.

Acknowledgement of that is necessary. That is what continues, so investment in the inner self is what is needed now. All other things are trivial. They are of no importance.

Prepare! Prepare!

Gain tranquility

In the peace, tranquility reigns for the spirit. Discover your peaceful place and be with the tranquil. In the peace you will discover much about yourself. You will always be nourished and the Light will shine ever more brightly with you.

So seek those moments of quiet and calm the mind, and gain tranquility. This will give you a great reward.

Nothing that is worthwhile happens without some degree of effort. So work quietly to gain this peace and tranquility.

Fun is important

Fun is very important and you need to have more fun in your life. Serious times are not always all that there is and fun releases so much more.

If you allow the fun to enter your life, the inner child will be so happy and the adult will grow.

Happiness helps

Quiet and calm and peace of heart. Happiness is a wonderful thing to embrace in your life. Happiness helps all aspects of life of the humankind. Allow this to reverberate in every part of you and you will be renewed and feel the renewal.

Release yourselves

Release yourselves from the bonds you place around you. These bonds are the restrictions you place upon yourselves and are created only by the mind and don't represent what you truly are.

Know that you are more than the mind. The spirit that dwells within holds knowledge and unconditional love, and therefore the purpose of your being.

Open yourself up to what drives your being and work with the inner knowings of your spirit, soul, essence – and be free.

Create your life anew. A life in touch with all that dwells within, where your potentialities abound with true purpose and unconditional love of self and all that there is.

Start each day this way.

Freedom

It is in the peace *(for example, when meditating)* that we will contact you. When you seek peace you find us.

It is in this space that you will find the greatest freedom and love.

Freedom allows you to be who you are. That doesn't mean to say that you have to be a 'prissy person'.

It means that you need to envelop all of your being. Be enthusiastic for life. Feel the joy that comes from truly living. Live your life from the heart and you will be the magnificent being of Light that you are.

Let go of what no longer serves you

Surrender all things you no longer need, all those things that serve you no more.

In doing this you will allow yourself to grow. You will find new things to give you pleasure, to enhance your life, to give you the growth that you need and to allow you to move on.

In balance

The Circle of the Light is with you tonight. The connection from within is united to the without so you are in union tonight.

Feel the balance that is with you now. This balance is how you would be best served in leading your lives, because then you are enriched with all of the things that you need and you will lack nothing. You have everything that you need within, when you are connected without.

Tapestry of life

Stitch every stitch of your tapestry of life and allow it to reflect who you are. Everything in balance. Everything just right. Fun, happiness, joy, experience, upsets – all are what make life.

Let your stitching start. Everyone with care, everyone just right. Because you're with the Light.

Meditation

In the silence of your space we come. We come to let you know that there is more to your being than you realise, and in the peace you sense us.

Listen to yourself. Feel what you can. Register our presence and we will manifest with you.

Let us be part of your lives. Let us help you.

All we wish to do is let you embrace the fullness of who you are.

Energy during meditation

You are energy. All are energy. All existence is energy.

In meditation you let go of your physical form. The busy mind is quietened. And you allow the pure energy that you are to be present.

So you will see, feel, sense and BE, the magnificent being of Light and love that you truly are.

When you accept and know that you are pure energy you will know the source of all creation is with you and that you are one.

Everyone you know or have ever known is part of your journey and eternally exist as energy. The physical form is not all that there is.

Energy

We have been listening to much talk about energy and energy is what you are. Energy is all that there is and the energy of life is God-given and flows from the Source of all energy to you.

This energy is pure and will provide all that you need. It is the finest energy and when you realise that energy is eternal, you will know you continue.

There is an exercise that we want Kay to do with you and it is prepared.

This exercise is available as a guided meditation on our CD 'Meditations for Spiritual Development'.

Absorb the energy

All energy of the finest is here with you all right now. Please absorb the energy – let it assimilate throughout your entire being as this will give you what you need right now – that is the freedom to be what you are.

In this energy you will be exactly what you are to be and you will achieve everything you need to. Do tune in to this vibration and you will reach the potential of your essence and you will shine out brightly and attract all who need to seek the Light.

Work with the finest of energies and you will have the freedom you seek – the 'form' without the body.

Preciousness of all life

You request my presence and that is very welcome.

I tell of the preciousness of all life. All life needs to develop, encouraged by those of the Light energy.

All will benefit from knowing the Light, and the Light is with those here and their associates in their lives.

Light is increasing

Surrender the spirit. Allow us to help. Trust always in the energy of the Light and you will receive all of the help you need. We are just a little way away.

We see the increase of Light on Earth and it is due to all who seek the Light, opening up.

This Light is increasing and the ascension times are rising and the wave of Light is increasing and enveloping so many, and it's all because of groups like this (our meditation group) that it is happening.

Please continue! Please spread yourself in love on those that you come in contact with.

We leave you with love and we leave you with peace.

Tree in spring

Like the tree that flourishes in the spring with new growth with hope for the future, you are. Allow the learning and give teaching, for all things will benefit. All people on the Earth will benefit from what can be given by channels of Light.

Everything comes to pass. Everything reaches its potential when there is a desire and the intention is right. Be your potential and give of the Light to all who seek.

Realising your spiritual gifts

Greetings! Love and Light is with you all.

Your help in realising your spiritual gifts raises the energy. It helps all in the Light as it helps all who you touch. The gifts are precious and it takes a long time for many on the Earth plane to realise that they have these gifts. We rejoice when we see them being accepted with humility and understanding.

Let the gifts work with and for you. They will bring much to you and they will do much for the heavens above.

Earth changes and transition

This section contains messages about changes that are happening to Mother Earth and humanity as we move towards a world based on love.

As mentioned earlier, many of these messages were addressed to our weekly meditation group, or 'circle' and need to be read with that in mind.

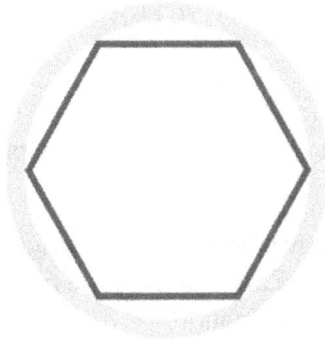

Preparation for transformation

Many are called as the work begins to move Earth into the energy of love. Much needs to happen for this to eventuate and we are working with many on the Earth plane.

Preparations already started will be strengthened and expanded to ensure Earth receives the much-needed energy for this transformation.

Towards a more loving community on Earth

The time on your calendar is about to eventuate when the energies will flow more freely, helping with the Earth's energy flow towards a more loving community on Earth.

Allow yourselves to accept that the energy will help your connection, bringing through more information to allow Earth's expansion.

Love energy heals

Love energy will heal at the very core of the being. This is where all healing needs to take place. The soul, spirit, essence will be loved and therefore nourished, become fertile and will be free to soar, it will be strengthened and know its purpose once again.

This allows you to show the love in your heart and transform not only yourself, but all who come in contact with you.

Show your Light and the love within your being as this will change your perspective on all aspects of your life. Let it be seen by others.

We, The Circle of The Light of The Love Energy – The God Force Energy – remind you that love is the purest energy form. Let us heal the spirit, soul, essence and allow Earth to enter another higher dimension.

The Great Magnificence

We see the love starting to flow. Small steps are being made and this is what will contribute to the whole.

Expansion of the Light will continue with the many that are already accepting of the words. The words of love, the words of Light. All of the kindness and understanding that brings the harmony is what we are seeing and we are so pleased.

Earth is moving forward, Earth is making progress, all people who help with this progress will feel the love shining in and through them, through their very being. This is such a wonderful step for mankind, humankind and the Earth.

There are great things that will start to flourish as the veil allows more to flow from spirit to spirit.

Allow the time of the Great Magnificence to be upon the Earth.

Life on Earth

All life is precious, as I have mentioned before.

As all spirits who enter the body come for a purpose, all come for quite specific reasons. Because the planet Earth is quite a challenging place, all have chances of leaving, not through their own hand – but maybe you would see it through illness, accidents, natural disasters, and those that cannot see their purpose being fulfilled would leave at that time. They would further discuss and enter into development on the side of the Light.

No spirit lives in the body without the opportunity of fulfilling their task. The spirit within can get, and does get, very frustrated when it feels its opportunities and purpose are being confined.

It is therefore very important when times are like this in the human life, for breaking free from that confinement to happen. The spirit within seeks in all things the opportunity to be that Light within and to develop and expand.

The earthly purpose can provide and will provide – but only when trust is applied and when the frustrations are known. Instead of acceptance of these frustrations and confinements, a way through needs to be found for the further expansion of the Light within – and this will give the human being the physical body opportunities and contentment.

World based on love

It is with much pleasure that I speak with you tonight.
There are great changes taking place.

The world based on love, as we have said, is the crucial
element of the change and the messages that we have
been giving are the instrument for the expansion. The
expansion of the soul, all souls, will allow the time of the
golden rain and a Great Magnificence upon the Earth.

All people who are awakened, and the soul seeks the
nurturing and the wisdom, create a connection of golden
thread that envelopes as it weaves its way around the
Earth, providing a barrier between the negative energies.

This barrier is so important. It needs to be woven thickly
and then the time of the golden rain will be upon the
Earth.

Change to be determined by us

The world as you know it is full of beauty and wealth. It is in need of much help from the humans who live there. Much understanding of the needs of the Earth, the world, is required now.

All events are with purpose. All love is to be released.

There is change. There will be more change. How much change will be determined by yourselves. Place all trust in what is asked.

Listen! All need to help. All need to love. All need to cooperate and be as one.

It is fundamental!

Earth will prevail

We come in peace and love and with hope for all of humanity. Events, which take place, are but what is expected and nothing to fear.

All of your energy of love needs to be raised and in the raising of this energy the Earth can and will prevail.

Compassion

Compassion is to be seen. All things that we see happening on your Earth we see with compassionate eyes. It would be good if all on Earth could show their compassion for one another and then there would be understanding – and not dissension on Earth.

Much is happening on Earth that is wholesome, but much is happening that is heart aching to us to see. Build bridges with one another, connect with one another on a link of understanding and tolerance, and much will be achieved.

The love energy that has been spoken about in many of the previous messages still needs to be raised on Earth and many incidences occurring at this time will raise the energy of love. But we don't want to keep seeing these things happen to Earth in order to allow the energy of love to flow.

Throughout the development of the Earth, many lessons have been given allowing growth. So do work to allow the love energy to flow so that the lessons do not need to be so severe.

Learn from the past. Civilisations were destroyed because of misuse – and rejuvenation of the new happened.

Work with one another. It is the answer – understanding, harmony, love.

Love is the key.

Unite to help Earth

This message was from a being that Kay had not previously channelled. He took some time to adjust to the energy before he started to speak.

Dense energy here. Quite hard for me.

Peter: Thank you for coming here my friend.

I am sent to help.

Kay stood up.

Much better, much better! Yes, well – there is much to talk about, much to talk about!

Heaven's helping. You all seem to be in so much distress and in much need of the help of the Wise Ones. Earth is suffering and adjusting to all of her demands and is needing to readjust in order to cope with the new energy that is all around.

The new energy will help Earth, but it will not happen straight away. Earth needs more help in adjusting to its new requirements. The help is coming through the channels of Light that are helping to direct the heaven-sent energies.

These energies will spread out from the channels and also penetrate the Earth, but connections to the heavens need to be made so that this energy force can flow. It needs to flow!

We have many people on the Earth who are conductors for us and the time is coming for them to all unite, on one night, to allow this charge of energy to help the Earth.

Earth is managing at the moment with its own readjustments, but the heaven-sent energies will be needed. The time is not right now, but is soon.

Enough to assimilate I think.

Peter: Thank you for coming, please come again.

We want to help! We need to help!

Gifts of knowledge

It is with much pleasure that we are welcomed here tonight to share our gifts of knowledge. There are times ahead when you will all need to express the wisdom of the heavens.

The heavens are full of all the knowledge and it is being transported through the Earthly channels at this time, and the Awakening and the time of the Great Magnificence will be upon the Earth.

Allow this to happen because it will benefit all who are ready. Please continue to let this energy come through because it is essential for the continuum of the Earth.

Dimensions changing

I am from a very distant place in your terms and your place of life is having to deal with many things in its universe at this time. We help.

The dimensions of your planetary system are changing.

Shine the Light

The universe that your Earth is in is going through a series of new gravitational pulls, which is causing it to draw on all its might to maintain its current thrust. There are many from without your universe activating energy adjustments to balance and they are ready to assist Earth more if it is unable to keep to its course. It is important to the Whole that the Earth's course be maintained.

Earth is responding to this situation and in doing so is releasing pressure and altering shape. The result is change for those that depend upon her, awakening in some new life patterns, thought patterns and belief systems.

It is all as it should be. The beings on Earth that conduct themselves from the heart and shine their Light are actually working for the balance of Earth. Please shine the Light ever so brightly.

Changes in our universe

I am from the outreaches of your planetary system. We come to speak with you about the changes in your universe.

Your universe is going through a tremendous change. There are pulls on it and the gravitational pull is causing it some distress. It is requiring all of its might to hold its position. With the help of us and many more there will be stability and balance for Earth.

In the change of Earth – it is opening up and reshaping and this reshaping is causing many of the inhabitants of the Earth plane to discover that there is a different place for them.

They are not to stay as they are. It is all arranged and with the help of the outer energies the Earth will be able to prevail. But the inhabitants of Earth need to play their part.

We are part of the encouragement of discovering the important part of the human being. It is this part of the human being that needs to be seen. It needs to be open and work from the innermost part to provide the love and the balance that is needed.

We say this to help. Not to frighten, but to help.

Rejoicing in heaven

The Light that you each shine is united in purpose and shines brightly, and we come willingly to help.

With each human being who commits to this path there is much rejoicing on our plane, because it allows the spreading of the Light into all parts of Earth that you are in touch with.

Your purpose is awakened and is happening.

Allow yourselves to acknowledge your worth and in acknowledging this you will serve your purpose.

Beam of energy

The beam of energy in the centre of the circle is for all of you to draw on. It is strong.

This force is upon the Earth. It is for all to feel and know. It is needed now as you prepare for the next year.

Nothing to fear, but feel and pull and encourage this energy in all of the things that you do.

This is how the energy that is needed on Earth will come – through you. Pass it on.

We care that you care

We care that you care to come to be here to link into the energy and discover your path.

It is with trust that you will develop. We will care for you with every step that you take on the path to find yourself.

You can trust us. We nurture the spirit. We live in the heart and all that is needed is here for you, with us.

Ascension times and Earth's atmosphere

The Ascension times are spoken about and they are not mysterious. It simply means that the energy is raising. The energy of good, the energy of Light, and the energy of love is being raised on the Earth plane.

This is the preparation time and it is proceeding well with much Light being extended from the Earth to the heavens. This energy is what has been called for, for a long time. As it has now been raised all things are going to plan.

There is more consideration required and it is about the atmosphere of the Earth. All human beings are responsible for the change that is needed.

The atmosphere is gaseous and Earth has to move within the gaseous atmosphere, and as human beings use the elements of Earth unwisely they create a problem and the Earth has to keep adjusting to all that is about it.

Consider the Earth, not just the people on the Earth. Consider the Earth!

Love Mother Earth

Love is the most important of human emotions. It is what is raising the amount of Light in humankind on Earth, allowing Light to shine from Earth for the first time.

This time is being called by many – the age of ascension. This energy of Light will continue to increase as more become awakened to the Light. Those who are already shining brightly will achieve this energy increase. It is heart-warming to see this awakening age unfold.

We encourage you to expand this awareness of love to your mother, Earth. Earth and humankind live in atmospheric conditions that provide all requirements. It is a union of existence so it is necessary for all to be in harmony with each other. Mother Earth is your provider, and you are her carers.

Earth lives in a universe of gaseous elements that provide her needs and yours. When the atmospheric balance is altered in any way, Earth has to make adjustments to maintain position within its universe of existence.

Many, many changes have been made by Earth, but only so much adaptation can be made.

Humankind needs to realise it needs to take on the role of 'carer' with seriousness to allow Earth to exist. Give back, nourish, consider, understand, be in harmony and love Earth to ensure its continuance. Remember to keep loving each other and love Mother Earth.

Currency of love

Be reassured that human beings that walk your Earth have been on many journeys before, each journey changing the level of their energy vibration. Human beings who are upon the Earth have all moved forward and exist in their achieved level of vibration.

Achievement of task in each incarnation may or may not occur, their life review on returning to spirit will decide this and set the scene for the next incarnation. So you can see that it is the Life Review that will prescribe the next learning.

All on Earth now want Earth to take its place in the universe. It may not seem like that to you, but all have a part to play – with each opposing action forming new definitive direction in the awakened.

Angels walk the Earth now in human form. For they have accepted the call to help Earth at this very special time in Earth's development, its reshaping, and with its vibrational standing within the universe. There are also human beings that have progressed their vibrational level who are assisting Earth.

There are many channels upon the Earth that are helping with the awakening of the most necessary currency for Earth – Love. There is rejoicing in the heavenly realms as the awakening times are happening and continuing, allowing a time of greatness for Earth.

The currency of love provides abundance for all.

Wave of energy

The Circle of The Light is with you all tonight and we ask that you unite with us always. We can give you all the guidance and help and love that is needed and this is what you need to do.

The wave of energy that is enveloping Earth is progressing at the right level and the crescendo of the love will take it further.

It will raise it on its next journey and this is what we ask that you help with.

Be there for us and we will be there for you.

Golden thread

Greetings! In love and Light we come tonight.

Connections to the heavens are with each. It penetrates through the crown chakra and flows into your body. It is a golden thread and it is the core of your being.

It is love. It is your essence. It is the purpose for existence and it is for sharing with all.

Allow this to happen because it will benefit all who are ready. Please continue to let this energy come through because it is essential for the continuum of the Earth.

Changes in humanity

There are always changes going on in your world. And in your daily life you accept them. Perhaps with protest sometimes, but life carries on.

Change in your physical bodies at this time is awakening the essence of your being. This change is bringing about a wonderful awareness of who you are.

Let it happen.

Let this growth happen so you will be ready to greet the coming days, as we all help you. This is a significant time for Earth. The significance is in the growth of its inhabitants.

Change for the positive

The implementation of the cooperation of the consciousness of humankind is allowing the infill of new energy into the beings that are awakened, and their structure will change for the positive.

They will be able to contain the energy and allow it to flow to others. It is a great time for the Earth when this happens.

With love I leave you.

11-11-11: *a day of significance*

On the eve of the 11-11-11, a time of alignment within the universe of Earth's existence. A day of significance within the universe.

Many days of alignment have been happening. Over recent times, have been the most.

This eve day, of the event of significance, will be the most important. It is the day of the One – the Oneness of All. It will lead on to the next significant time in the 2012 year that is spoken about so often in your circles today.

But tomorrow is a great day for the universe.

Create heaven on Earth

Bring unto yourselves what it is that you believe that you will have in heaven and live a life of fullness on Earth. Fullness of consciousness.

Take on the new energy

It is with much love that we come to be with you all tonight.

The Light upon the Earth at this time is magnificent. It has aligned with all of the universe and all is well on Earth.

Take in the New Energy. It is there in abundance for you. It will help you move to another level in your development and in the development of Earth.

Take on the Energy!

Live your lives consciously

Live your lives consciously. Consciously live your lives. Awakened ones know of the spirit. They know to work with it. But we encourage all to work with spirit and to quieten the mind. The mind is not to take over the spirit. The spirit has all.

The spirit is what is needed and together the spirit and mind – second is the mind – you will live your lives consciously, bringing unto yourselves everything that you desire that is for the good of the Whole. For all are part of the Whole, and it is important that now that this new energy is upon the Earth, that this inflow continues into the beingness of humankind.

Help all to know that they are of one spirit, everyone united, one consciousness.

Please help the heavens more. It is not over. There is rejoicing in the heavens and there is rejoicing in the universe, but it is necessary to continue with the flow of the love. This is so important – to keep the energy flowing. Let the wave continue and build so that all are ready as the months approach to 2012.

Please continue. Please help us.

It is important not to stop, not to think that all has been achieved. We do appreciate what has happened, but it needs to continue.

The Light of the Lord is upon you and all on Earth. In love we go. In love all will be known.

Absorb the new energy

Let the Light be the governance of your life and let the Light lead you into receiving the *new energy* that is upon the Earth.

This energy is so special and it will give you the ability to move dimensionally. And it is a gradual process. You need to have time to receive it.

So make as much time available to sit in the peace and receive.

It is here for you.

Please make time. Please receive.

Wings of angels

The wings of the angels are around all in this room tonight. Feel the gentleness of their vibration penetrate and love the spirit within.

Within each of you are gifts from the heavens and they are yours to work with and share. The gifts are very special. Accept them. Use them and treasure them for they are yours to awaken others.

Accept with love.

Under our care

Energy that is created in groups like this provide us, the group that works through Kay – and there are many others, but it provides us with an opening to speak and give love and give advice.

We seek these openings as the people who inhabit the Earth are *under our care* and we wish to help. It is of our very essence – it is from us – a need to help.

Place your existence in love and then your existence will be whole and will be fulfilled.

Provide openings for us to come and help. Help from the heavenly realms will assist your being.

A thank you

Your circle is enclosed with pure white light. All of you here are connected to the energy that is building in the centre of your group.

All life is precious and you are all, ours to care for. Your preciousness is the commitment to the connection, that allows you to stand in the Light.

Your Light shines and attracts us each time and we just want to thank you for being so willing to learn and help – help the Earth and help the heavens.

Energy that comes through the circle

All energy that comes through the circle is from a divine source full of love, encouragement to continue with the development of the spirit, soul, essence of the being. Please continue.

Message for lightworkers

Oh precious ones who have lit the Light within the heart of the human form. We thank you.

In this special time please send your love to all that you meet. Your energies will uplift many and the guidance that you have now within will help Earth.

You are dear ones. All are dear ones to the realms of the Light. Please remember – do not forsake the Light.

Caretakers of the Light

This is a wonderful time on your Earth. A time of Light, much Light. Rejoice because you have created an environment to allow the Light to penetrate all. This Light is the Light of love and it is our most precious thing to give the Earth.

We are the caretakers of the Light and it is our mission to pass on this love, this Light, this energy that can create for you all that you desire. What you desire in love, in true love, will manifest and it will bring peace to you, all you know, and the Earth.

And Earth will be secure, for all of the Light creates the Earth's position in the atmosphere of the universe.

Energy of Love

Energy of love is so precious. It is the gift from the heavens and it is upon the Earth for all to take nourishment and feel the precious love around them. This time on Earth is given for all to feel this energy. This energy will help all who seek. Those who seek can pass this energy to those that they know and awaken them to what the possibilities are on Earth.

Earth is a beautiful planet, it is a beautiful place to live, but it needs to be given all of the nutrients it can and these need to come from the human beings who inhabit the Earth. They have the gifts of love. They have the knowledge. They just need to wake up and use it.

There are things happening in your planetary system, and they are all meant to be, but they need not be catastrophic to Earth because the Earth beings know they need to help.

Awaken all that you can because in awakening those others Earth can be given all it needs. It is not up to one person to do this. It is up to all who seek to take onboard their tasks of the ripple effect and spread the words of love, the guiding words of love.

Beauty

It is with much pleasure that we come again to be with you all.

We wish you to know that you are beauty – beauty that is connected without. When you expose the beauty of your being you will be connected and you will know all of the universe's secrets.

So embrace your beauty and let it out. Let it be seen by everyone. It is your magnificence. It is the Light.

Let the beauty out.

Offer empathy

Awaken the sensitivity centre within your being, the centre of awareness that has come to you through your many experiences in life.

All of these experiences will allow you to connect with others through empathy. Offer your empathy as a listening ear and with an understanding nod. Do not dominate, allow their story to unfold.

• Be comforting not smothering.

• Be supportive.

• Be understanding.

• Become a friend.

Remember they need to work through their events just like you. Allow them to seek within and discover their inner wisdom and beauty so they heal. Let them lay the foundation for their sensitivity centre to offer empathy to those in need.

Find the answers within

Many seek to be given the answers about what is to happen in this the 2012 year that Earth finds itself in. But the answers are within and they will not be given from without. They need to be discovered within. All that we can do is give guidance and advise how to find the within.

It is not the task of heaven to give all of the answers, because you are here to discover for yourself.

Please find the answers within. They are there, they need to be recognised and they need to be worked with and then the beauty of your world will be discovered.

Open up to the possibilities of having a wonderful existence on the Earth plane. It is not difficult to have. It is available to all. And then, then everything will be realised.

Give your answers in all of your expressions, all of your actions and all of your words. Give the answers and give the actions of love.

It is not hard. It is to consider yourself as a beautiful being of Light and love and to see everyone else in that way too. Is that so hard for you all to do?

Discovery of yourself

Dear ones who walk the Earth plane are walking the plane with the Light within, and your presence and being is known by me so very well.

If you consider that the Light dwells within you then you will realise the preciousness of your being. And you will be able to know and love yourself and you will be able to love others. This is what is asked and this is what you can do.

And when you can see yourself as the Light that walks the Earth, then you will know your true beauty and you will help and love others. This is what is needed in your world and this discovery of yourself will do what needs to be done in the 2012 year on Earth. We ask that this is activated this year.

We cannot be any more clear. We cannot run your lives. We cannot run your Earth. That is your task. That is why you are here. We know you can help. We know you are helping and this is your mission – complete this task, and what needs to be done on Earth will be done.

We cannot tell you any more. You must discover your core.

Task of all channels on Earth

I have come to join you tonight. I represent The Circle of The Light and our energy is all about you. You know you are energy. You know you exist in energy and this time on the Earth is a time of very high energy.

This energy is new and it is coming through because of what has been happening between Earth and heaven – the arrangements that are working between Earth and heaven.

This is a very fine precious, energy and it is available to all at this time. This energy will raise your vibration. It will meet the heavens and you will be fulfilled. Your vibration will be such that you can help Earth and heaven and you will bring to Earth the love, the energy that is desired on Earth because it is what all Earth beings cry out for.

It is what they want more than anything, but they don't open their hearts sufficiently to receive the energy and that is your task. That is the task of all channels on Earth at this time.

Feel the energy that is here now. That is the energy that you are. That is the energy that is available for all. Please pass it on. Let Earth know heaven in this 2012 year.

More about the new energy

The Circle of The Light has joined you again tonight and we wish to continue to talk about the new energy that is upon the Earth at this time.

This energy is for all, as we have said. It is the best of energy and it is coming through to fill the human being, to let it know its truth.

Let this energy permeate your being when you are in this sort of (*meditation*) group because the energy is particularly strong, and we are bringing it through for you all. This energy will help you realise your being and it will help you to help others. This is our wish.

Let it happen. Do not stop the energy. It is what is awaited on the Earth plane.

From love to love

It is in love that you come (to Earth).

From love you come, to love you will return. If you can return as love, then complete you will be.

The time you spend upon the Earth is a time for you to grow. It is a time for you to be who you truly are, the Light within you.

This is a task you are all given. It is a task we urge you to complete. Be Light and Love on the Earth. Be compassionate to all that you see, and all that you know, and let your essence be.

So when it is time to return to love, you will love be.

Joy in your heart

We come again tonight, as we want you to know that the Light in your heart needs to be full of joy. Joy that will touch the world. Joy that will give you nourishment.

And let this Light in the heart connect with all of your being – the physical, the mental and the spiritual, and let your potential be vast.

Stand fast in the Light and be your true self.

Your energy

I stand forward and bring through the *energy of love*. You know this energy. This is the energy from which you come. Your energy still dwells from where you came and we know it very well.

Your energy within your human form is beautiful and rich and has everything that you need to help you on your way, to help you to Light the path for all that you come in contact with. The beam of Light that is with each of you is a collective Light and it joins you all together. It is the Light of Love.

Let this be what you will be on Earth. Let the people you come in contact with know you as we do. You have the most beautiful energy, so please release it. Please show it and let that beam from Earth return to the heavens above where we dwell and where you have dwelt with us and you are still with us. Never forget it.

You live dimensionally

You live dimensionally. This is for some a new concept. So to those we impart this information.

Your energy is in your human form and we have said it is with us too. So if you can accept this, then stretch a little more.

If you can accept that, then consider please that it is also possible, for your energy to be in other parts of the universe experiencing other existences too. These run parallel. A multiplicity of your energy exists.

Remember your energy is divine, it is within you and without – so is in everything that is.

In your quieter times you may have awareness of what exists without. This awareness will stretch you to explore further in your human existence, providing expansion that benefits the Whole.

Love yourself

In love we come as always, and we surround your group tonight, and we want you to feel the words we say. Not just with your ears.

We come to tell you, you need to love yourselves. You cannot give love until you love yourself.

You have this energy available to you now. It is all nurturing. It is what you need, but there is no point us just saying this. We need you to feel it.

You need to love yourselves. Love yourselves, forgive yourselves.

You are what you are and you are beautiful and whole and everything that you need to be.

Just honour yourself.

Love yourself — part 2

Loving yourself, we have spoken to you about. It is a very necessary part of development.

The human being gathers around itself layers as it moves through its life journey. If the layers are such that they are protecting against the truth, they will not help.

It is necessary to peel back the layers exposing the truth of who you are and the love that you are.

Believe in yourselves. Be love.

The veil continues to thin

I come in peace and I come in love and I come to tell you that the veil continues to thin between our world and yours. The Light streams in, connecting with the Light channels and allowing work of good to happen on the Earth plane.

There is one common thing that connects all humankind, and that is love. It is the purpose for your being. It is like the triangle, it pulls together the three elements to bring oneness. Love is the core of all things on Earth.

If you complete this task of raising love on Earth then your heart will be so complete and it will rejoice in heaven.

Visit the dimension of the Light

Oh, what wonderful energy is with you tonight! We have brought the Light. It streams in and it nourishes you. If you feel it at the heart you can move from where you sit to where we are and you can experience the dimension of the Light.

Do this when you come as you will improve your connections and you will experience the dimension of love. You will leave your heavy feet behind and you will soar and realise that there is so much more.

Feel, feel with your very being and then you are all that you are.

No separation

Manifestation of the Light that you shine to us tonight is so welcome. It is beautiful and we remind you to keep it shining.

Know your blessings in life and give thanks for them. This will help you to grow more. When you appreciate what you are, you will light up.

You are one with the Light. There is no separation in your being. You are united with the Light.

Let it be.

Oneness

Move closer to the part of you called spirit and become in harmony with the Source. This harmony is unity and the unity is oneness, and that is all that there is.

In oneness, your heart – the essence of you – will be the operating centre and the Light will be. You will be in appreciation of all that you are.

You will be able to move and feel more than the third dimension in which you experience your life.

Ensure you give yourself a daily gift of peaceful time to experience the joy of being Light.

Spiritual poetry

Sometimes Kay wakes up in the morning with the first line of a poem in her mind. When she writes down the first line the rest just flows onto the paper. As Kay has never written any sort of verse before, she believes this writing is being channelled from her guides.

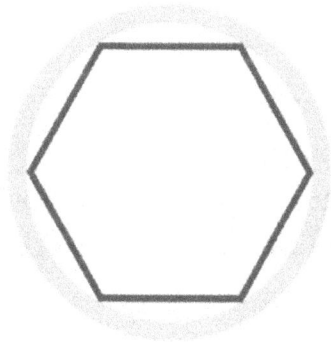

Present our plan

Around you we stand
So you can feel our guiding hands
As we want you to know it's time to activate our plan
On our behalf you will stand and present our plan.

Parable of the birds

I sit and watch the birds at play
From behind my tinted window pane
And from my vantage point I see
But they don't see me.

The birds they sing and hop and play
They squabble and jostle on the feeding tray
They eat for themselves and for others they take away
And when all in the tray is gone they fly away.

The birds still sing and hop and play
But are no longer seen from my window pane.

When

When eyes see beauty
And ears hear laughter
When the senses are awakened to the day's fresh fragrances
When mouths speak only kind and guiding words
When arms embrace
When hands help
When fingers no longer point
When legs march only for peace
When feet dance in joy
When minds unite to create good
And there is respect for all
Then the heart and soul will sing with love.

Healers unite with the Light

Healers unite tonight
Be channels for the Light
To deliver much needed sight
To the seekers of the Light.

Unite with the Light tonight
The seekers of the Light
Be awakened to your might
So you can always live in Light.

Awakened to the Light
You gain special sight
To see the true delights
At one with the Light, all is right.

Morning

In the morning
Choose your dawning
And deliver unyielding
Your essence revealing
Your love – and be truly appealing.

In love – when you are truly appealing
You will attract all right dealings
And bring unto yourself all needed feelings
Ensuring all healings
To expand your love and be more truly appealing.

When love is expanding
It is really rewarding
Not only for you, but those quietly urging
" Be from the heart, be your calling"
Because then, you will be most truly appealing.

Let me guide you

Dance with me in the moonlight tonight
Feel my embrace, so gentle yet tight
Let me guide you in this dance – called life
And move in rhythm, as one, tonight.

Dance with me in the moonlight tonight
Feel joy and happiness for life ignite
Let this flame for life spread much Light
As we move in rhythm, as one, tonight.

Dance with me in the moonlight tonight
Feel adventure and courage for life alight
Let your lodestar guide you aright
As we move in rhythm, as one, tonight.

Dance with me in the moonlight tonight
Feel wisdom and knowledge infuse your might
Let this flow in all your dealings in life
As we move in rhythm, as one, tonight.

Dance with me in the moonlight tonight
Feel my love and know you're just right
Let this be your power to abundance in life
As we move in rhythm, as one, tonight.

Angels of the Light

The Angels of the Light
Give to you a star, so bright
To illuminate your darkest night
And watch over your special life.

The Angels of the Light
Send you healing beams of Light
To ensure you're fit and right
So you will soar to great heights.

The Angels of the Light
Walk with you day and night
To enhance your life with love and Light
So you will know you are Light.

The Angels of the Light
Proclaim in melodies of delight
You are beings of divine Light
And are free to BE by divine right.

Your lodestar

I am the lodestar of your life
When you work with me there will be no strife
Anything I say through you will be just right
And what is needed in life.

Time to shine

It is time for you to shine
To attract those who seek to align
To the energy so pure and fine
That unites the spirit with the divine.

Fusion with the divine
Will nurture the spirit for all time
Empowering with love sublime
Another prism of the Light to shine.

Each prism of Light magnifies and defines
The purpose of heaven on Earth to outshine
For life is love and love is life divine
So those aligned will always, always shine.

I am the spirit within

When you look in a mirror
The reflection you see is not really me
It is merely the human form you see
I am the spirit within, the essence of thee
Please find and treasure me.

When you find me
I can help you be all that you can be
I am love, I am perfect and whole
For I am divine you see
And that is how you too can be
When you find and treasure me.

I have been with you for all time
And when you acknowledge me
You will know your purpose and at one be
United we'll shine and reflect the source divine
So when you look in the mirror of life
You will see me.

11-11-11 *verse*

We hear you ask, what is happening today?

Well the universe aligns this day
To the energies from far away
Ensuring Earth a passageway
Within the White Light Ray.

Celebrate this wonderful day
Earth now rides the love energy sway
And the universe welcomes it to stay
Within the White Light Ray.

All elements unite this day
Earth, humankind and the heavens say
Earth comes of age this day
At one with the White Light Ray.

Love is the Key

Reap before you sleep

Before you sleep
We ask that you reap
The wisdom of our speak
Because we divulge what you seek.

Christmas message

Christmas is about to be celebrated this year
With family and friends that you hold dear
But is the purpose of this celebration clear
Or is it seen only as a way to gain more gear?

Foster the meaning true this Christmas time of year
The remembrance of the baby Jesus dear
The gift of love given for all to know and share
So that humanity would no longer need to fear.

You see Christmas is a 'Giving' time of year
And a time for all to be full of joy and cheer
For the love and hope given that first Christmas time year
So celebrate this gift so unique and rare.

Spare no cost this Christmas time of year
Give the most precious, priceless gifts you have to share
The gifts of Love and Hope to those you hold dear
For these are real treasures to be enjoyed in every year.

Love, happiness and peace

Where there is love, there is happiness
Where there is happiness, there is love.

And where there is love, there is peace
Where there is peace, there is hope.

Hope for a future of love, happiness and
peace.

The Creator's breeze

The trees stir in graceful movement from the Creator's breeze
Awakening sounds of nature to float in the air with ease
Gentle is the voice that calls for you to hear and heed
So listen, for the sounds that float in the air with ease.

The trees stir in graceful movement from the Creator's breeze
Manifesting visions of unity to be seen with ease
Beautiful is the sight shown for you to see and heed
So watch for visions of unity that can be seen with ease.

The trees stir in graceful movement from the Creator's breeze
Yielding an abundant bounty to be enjoyed with ease
Luscious is this nourishment for you to have and heed
So take nurture from the bounty that can be had with ease.

The trees stir in graceful movement from the Creator's breeze
Showing that when harmony exists, there is ease
Empowering your being with all that you need
Your tree of life stirs, empowered, ready to reign and please.

The 2012 year

The 2012 year is here
So let the beauty of your time appear
Let the Light so rare
And love so dear
Be manifest in you and all those for whom you care.

So ask through prayer
That you discover this year
That what you are is clear
So Light and love on Earth appear
In this much awaited year.

United in love will steer
Proclamation of the gifts you bear
And the golden rain will be here
So the Great Magnificence will appear
Connecting you to the one who cares.

The key

Turn the key
And discover me
The Light within thee.

Then you will see
What you will truly be.

Crystalise your reality

Do you have clarity of your reality?

Your reality crystalises the nearer you get to your spirituality

As then you know there is no duality

Oneness is all that there is in reality.

The gift

Upon the Earth he came and walked

He played, he learnt, and then about love he taught

He revered his Father and his given task in faith sought

He gave of himself so love would be in all who on the Earth
walked

So special is the gift he gave, when accepted will welcome
in a new age

Accept, accept and bring to be the love in thee and all
that be.

Spirit guides

We are a spirit temporarily inhabiting a physical body. Most of us have been here on Earth in many previous lives. The purpose of us coming here to the physical plane is to learn many lessons, which will contribute to our spirit's ongoing spiritual development.

Each time we incarnate on Earth we are assisted by a number of invisible spirit helpers of the Light. We each have a main guide who is with us for life and likely was our main guide in some of our previous lives.

The main guide's task is to assist the individual to accomplish their life's work or purpose. There are also a number of other spirit guides who are there from time to time to help us with particular things. The main guide also acts as a gatekeeper so that only other appropriate spirit helpers may be given access.

Guides generally cannot do anything for us unless we ask for their help. They only provide positive guidance. We have free will and they are not allowed to do anything that would control us.

Spirit guide drawing

The spirit guide picture on the cover was drawn by psychic artist Rachel Auton. Rachel ran a meditation group that Kay had attended in 2008. During this time Kay started to see the features of a man, just the nose and eyes. Then Rachel moved to Australia and we lost contact. When Kay joined another meditation group, gradually the whole face appeared along with a further two guides, one male and one female.

Recently, Kay found Rachel's website and regained contact. Kay arranged for Rachel to draw one of her spirit guides and this picture is the result. Mary's face with the veil over the hair, is exactly what Kay has been seeing through her third eye. Rachel had no knowledge of Kay's guides before doing the drawing.

Rachel also does a psychic reading for her client when doing the drawing. Here is an excerpt from Rachel's reading for Kay, which explains the process used.

" Normally I would just tune in to a person's energy (by looking at a photograph that clients are asked to supply) and ask a guide to step forward, but in your case I held onto your book (*Earth Messages of the Love Energy*) and asked 'The Circle of The Light of The Love Energy' to present themselves. What I saw was blinding light of golden yellow/white and what appeared to be stars. I feel this collective consciousness difficult to draw as a human interpretation, so I waited and then a spokesperson stepped forward and that was Mary, Queen of the Angels, otherwise known as Mother Mary."

For further information about Rachel Auton, energy worker, teacher and psychic artist go to www.lotuslifestyle.com.

Rachel's website contains a fascinating gallery of many of the spirit guide pictures she has drawn.

The quietly-spoken female spirit guide that Kay often channels.

About the authors

Kay Meade is a trance medium who has been channelling messages from the 'Circle of The Light of The Love Energy', a group of spiritual beings, since mid 2009.

Kay and husband Peter Ashley practice and teach Reiki in New Zealand.

For further information about the authors, their books and meditation CDs, and the latest messages from The Circle of The Light of The Love Energy go to www.earthmessagepress.com.

The authors welcome any feedback or questions related to this book at www.earthmessagepress.com/contact-us.

Books by the authors include:
Earth Messages of the Love Energy
Poems for You

By the same authors

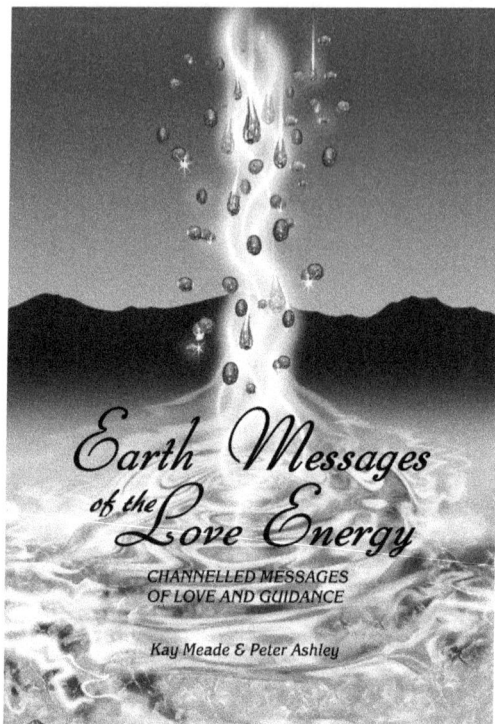

Earth Messages of the Love Energy, published in March 2011, is available from amazon.com in paperback and Kindle e-book formats.

It is also available as an e-book from the Apple iBookstore for iPad and iPhone, and from Barnes and Noble for the Nook e-book reader.

The following pages contain a few samples of the messages contained therein.

Love energy

The world is going through a great time of change and needs to know about Love Energy. Love Energy needs to be passed on, but before you can pass it on it needs to be understood and recognised.

Every person carries this energy, but not everyone is awakened to it. This energy is of your very essence, it is central to all that you are.

Awaken the soul's craving – be love by being from the heart. Every action, every word, every thought needs to be expressed in love.

Love is never given as a reward. Love is. Love is, it has no boundaries, it has no conditions.

The Light is love. Live your lives from the heart, then your love will be expressed. Be a disciple of the Light; show this Love Energy by living from the heart. Open your hearts to the Light, then the Love Energy is awakened.

The Light

Light is all that is needed. Realise that the Light is within and without you, so love yourself and love all that is about you. Feel the harmony – it radiates from the Light.

The Light is peace, and the Light gives all that is needed. Reach out for the Light always – embrace the Light and feel the harmony. The soul needs the love, it needs the peace and it needs the harmony that comes from the Light.

Open yourselves to this Light. You are the Light – remember you are always the Light. You are One, you are the Light. Feel the Oneness – be at one with the Light. Unite with the Light!

Your heavenly family

Every person living on Earth is born into a family. Collectively and individually, all have a part to play. Although when of age and therefore can fend for oneself, you should never think on your own as there is a collective consciousness – another family – you are part of a heavenly family.

Make a conscious decision to link to your heavenly family. Then work together – that is how everything is achieved.

The collective consciousness – it is when you remember to be part of the Whole. You have a family and it is not just here on Earth. It is all around you, it is within you.

When all allow their feelings to be from their highest self and therefore be from their essence, they will ignite and unite with the higher consciousness. The more people who know that their being is more than flesh and bone, the more people that awaken their spirit, soul, essence, the more who can connect into the greater consciousness, then more Light can be radiated from the heavens to the Earth.

Illumination is what is needed and this comes from the energy of The Circle of The Light.

In the *Meditations for Spiritual Development CD* we pass on two of the messages from The Circle of The Light of The Love Energy, in the form of guided meditations.

The CD is available from amazon.com.

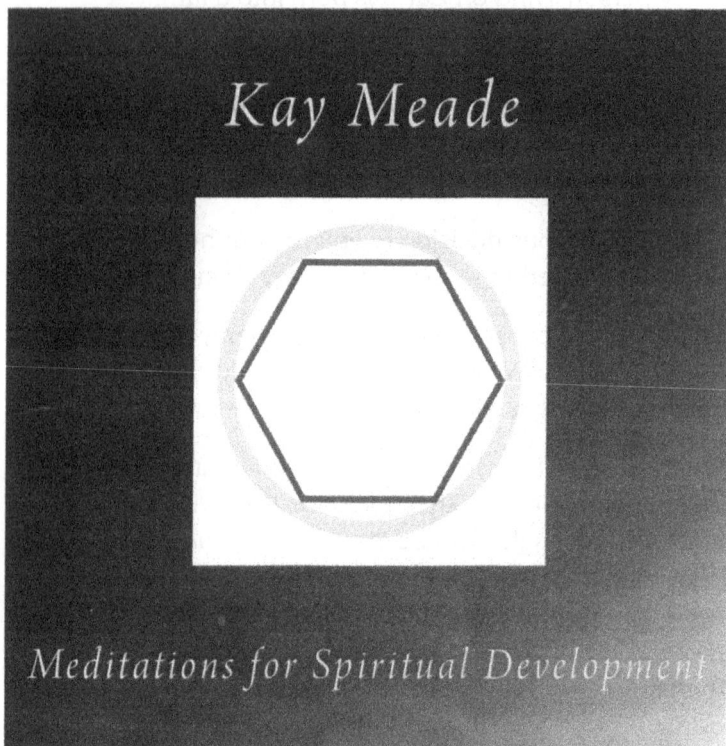

Kay Meade

Meditations for Spiritual Development

www.ingramcontent.com/pod-product-compliance
Lightning Source LLC
Chambersburg PA
CBHW061732020426
42331CB00006B/1216